Kisha Pollard & Chad Brown

The Smile in MY Voice

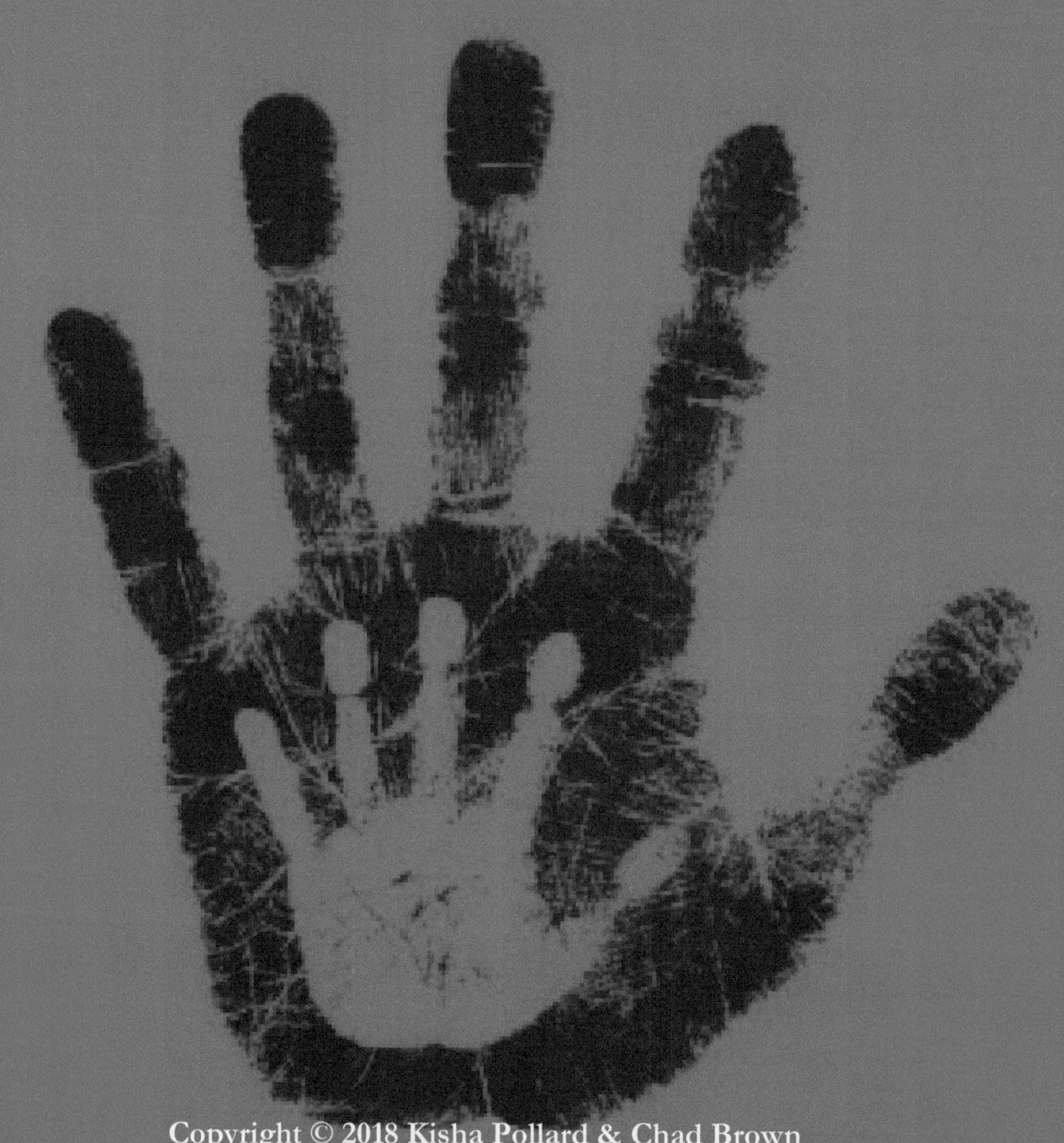

Copyright © 2018 Kisha Pollard & Chad Brown
All rights reserved.
ISBN: 0692058389
ISBN-13: 978-0692058381

~~Dedication~~

Special thanks and love to Kyairrah, Shaquoya, Mya, and Arabella for their contributions to this book and our lives.

My Life began the day you were born, or should I say it felt as if my life *officially* began the day you were born.

We're Expecting

I remember the moment I saw you for the first time. My heart had a new feeling. This was a feeling I had never felt before; a father's love. I knew that my life would never be the same.

You were created for an amazing purpose.

Our life together began. You were on a journey of learning and growing. While I got to be the luckiest man alive with the privilege of being by your side, lovingly guiding you through it all.

Be thankful for all things.

I was so excited to tell everyone you were finally here! I made sure to show everyone exactly how beautiful you were. I was definitely a proud dad.

Make every day your best day.

You began to grow up so fast. I remember your first birthday like it was yesterday. I couldn't believe that 365 days had past. You had teeth, knew how to walk and talk; well maybe a little bit.

Nothing can stop the greatness you have inside of YOU.

From the very first day you were born I would hold you in my arms, hum our favorite song until you fell asleep, and kissed you goodnight. We eventually added the ritual of reading several books each night.

You can do anything you set your mind to accomplish.

We've created lots of memories; your first trip to the beach, first slumber party, and learning how to ride your big girl bike.

Your light will brighten up dark places.

You showed me exactly how mature you were on the first day of school. You climbed on the big yellow bus, waved goodbye, and whispered to me, "I got this Dad".
That wouldn't be the last time you would say those words to me.

You are intelligent and possess great ideas.

There were also valuable lessons you learned. I remember the day you came home from school and you weren't smiling. You shared that some kids were not being nice, and they were making fun of you.

I put you on my lap, looked you in the eyes, and told you that everything would be okay. I made sure you knew that you were perfect in every way, and I asked you to promise to never forget that fact.

Love in its perfect form feels like magic.

Once a month we'd have our FUN FRIDAY! This was a day we dedicated to do something fun for just the two of us. It was our special father/daughter time.

We attended high school football games, went bowling, grabbed many ice cream cones, and went to the movies (the drive-in was our favorite). One time we allowed mom to join us and she captured one of my favorite pictures of us. This became our tradition and a time we cherished every month.

Quality time together creates experiences that makes long lasting memories.

The years continued to pass swiftly. There were a series of firsts; first dance, first plane ride, and YES, getting your driver's license. Some of these milestones I was not ready for you to experience. However, I knew the rites of passage must be part of your maturity.

I was in fact, impressed at how you handled these life events with such grace and elegance. You never appeared rattled, well not too much. My love for you was overwhelming.

You have permission to be exactly who you think you should be.

You were excited to get your first job. You had such energy and excitement every day you went to work. I happily accompanied you to deposit your first paycheck into your bank account. Of course, our next stop after the bank was the mall.

Always love yourself.

Now, you have finally made it! You achieved one of life's largest accomplishments; you graduated from high school. I beamed with pride and fought back the tears because I knew you'd be leaving for college very soon. We had a huge celebration, JUST FOR YOU; daddy's not so little girl!

You have the ability to conquer all obstacles you face.

Fall came, and it was time for you to start your college years. I drove you to the college campus, and it became one of our most memorable adventures.

We stopped for milkshakes, played some basketball, and finally made it to your dorm. I brought the last box to your room and knew I had to say goodbye. As I was leaving, you said a comforting and familiar sentence, "I got this Dad".

You are beautiful, creative and tremendously loved.

I knew this day would come, but I didn't want to accept it. You called to tell me that you had met a boy, and you believed you were in love. Your announcement made me feel uneasy, but I understood that every princess will eventually meet her prince.

You are worth more than the biggest pot of gold at the end of any rainbow.

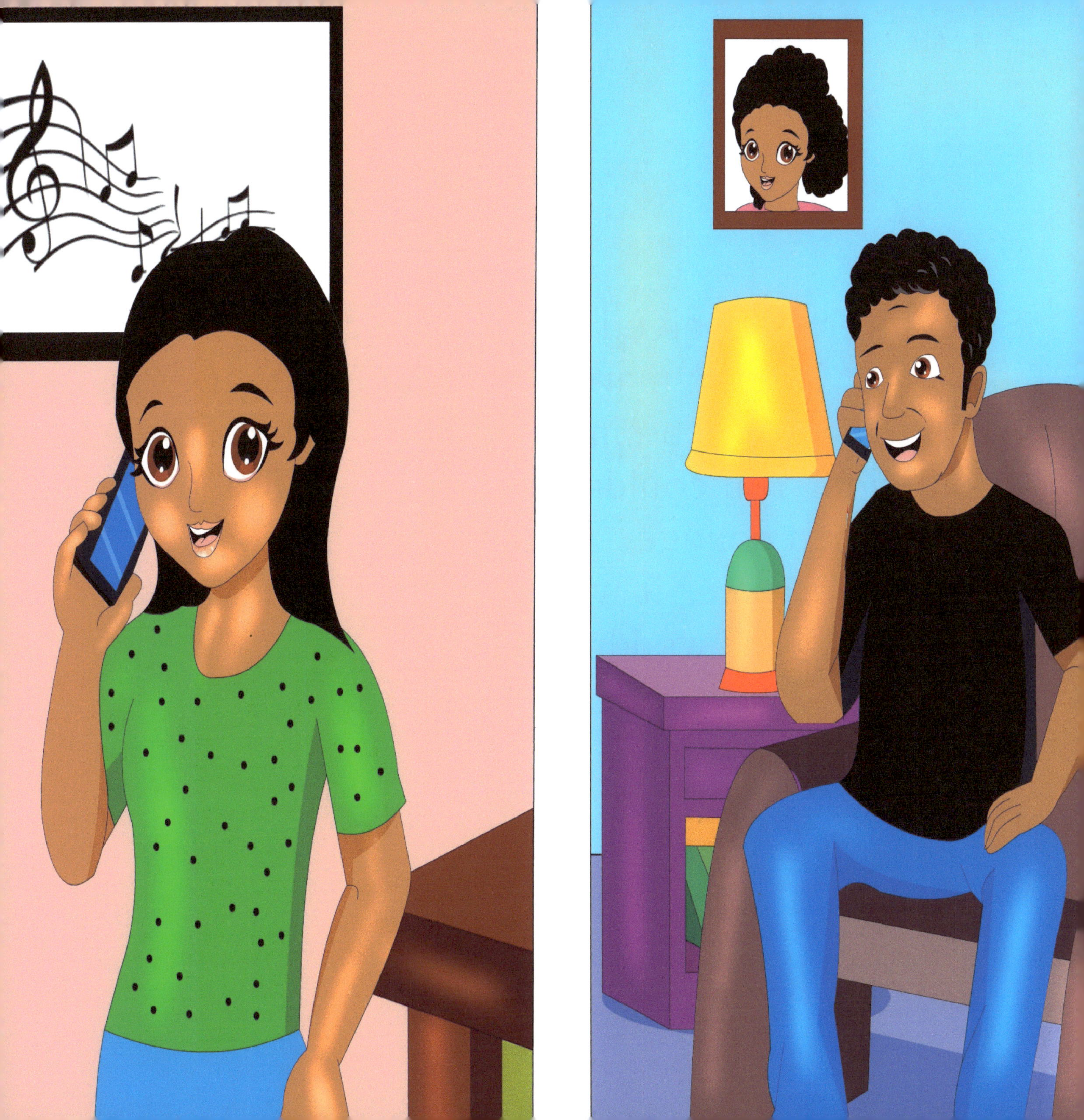

Soon after, I received a call asking if I would give your hand in marriage. Just like that, you were engaged to be married but with one Dad stipulation. You couldn't get married until you had finished college. Graduation came, and shortly thereafter it was time for the next big life event; your wedding day.

Being diligent and working hard will pay off.

You were an absolutely stunning bride. This was another moment in my life I was extremely proud and excited to call you my daughter. I realized you had become a woman, but I knew in my heart you would always be my little girl.

Before we walked down the aisle, I began humming our favorite song, and I gave you a kiss on your forehead. I felt exactly as I had when I first saw you.

Always know that in the end, everything will be alright.

You are now starting a new journey with the second luckiest man in the world; of course, I'm the first. Nothing can remove the smile from my voice when I think about the love I have for you.

You will forever be the smile in my voice.

I would not change one moment of our lives together. You will always be the sunshine on my rainy days, and will forever be the smile in my voice.

- You were created for an amazing purpose!!
- Be thankful for all things.
- You can do anything you set your mind to accomplish.
- Make every day your best day.
- Nothing can stop the greatness you have inside of YOU.
- Your light will brighten up dark places.
- You are intelligent and possess great ideas.
- Love in its perfect form feels like magic.
- Quality time together creates experiences that makes long lasting memories.
- You have permission to be exactly who you think you should be.
- Always love yourself.
- Rainy days allow us to appreciate the sunny days even more.
- You have the ability to conquer all obstacles you face.
- You are beautiful, creative and tremendously loved.
- Always know that in the end, everything will be alright.
- You are worth more than the biggest pot of gold at the end of any rainbow.
- Being diligent and working hard will pay off.
- You are the smile in my voice.

Thoughts from our GIRLS..

2 Years Old

♥   Running is fun.

♥   Counting is fun.

♥   I make my mommy and daddy fun.

10 Years Old

♥   There are less unicorns and more cupcakes.

♥   If you're not smiling, you're doing it wrong.

♥   You get more traits like courage, creativity, and you also gain more responsibility.

16 Years Old

- ♥   Failure is a part of succeeding.

- ♥   Smiling is a major key to happiness.

- ♥   Forgive but don't forget.

21 Years Old

♥   Hard work always pays off.

♥   Create your own destiny.

♥   Never doubt yourself.

www.ingramcontent.com/pod-product-compliance
Lightning Source LLC
Chambersburg PA
CBHW042004150426
43194CB00002B/119